The Charmed Garden
Second Edition

A Guide to Herb Gardening
By Judi Strauss

The Charmed Garden
Second Edition

Copyright © 2013 by Judi Strauss
All rights reserved.

ISBN 9781626130043
Library of Congress Control Number: 2013933399

Published by ATBOSH Media ltd.
Cleveland, Ohio, USA

www.atbosh.com

Disclaimer

Information on the purported medical attributes of any herbs described in this book is being passed on to you for informational purposes only. Neither the author nor the publisher advise or prescribe herbs for any medical purpose. Please check with your doctor or health care provider as to whether any of the herbs described in this book are of medical value to you. Also, consumption of certain herbs described in this book may be inappropriate for persons with certain physical conditions.

The author and publisher assume no liability for any omissions or for the use or misuse of the information contained in this book.

Acknowledgements

The author would like to acknowledge the following people for their help and support in the production of this book; Dr. Peter Gail, Dale Gallis, Jared Bendis, Martha Merrick Shaw, Jack Kerrigan, Rita Burke, Irene and Henry Strauss.

This book is lovingly dedicated to the memory of Ruth Stevens for sharing with me her love of plants. She taught a child the beauty of the world around her and that knowledge sustains me still.

Preface

Herbs have held a fascination for me for as long as I can remember. Their beautiful foliage and fragrance has always held a certain charm for me, a sort of magic. These are plants that thrive on a minimum of care yet reward us year after year with an abundant, flavorful harvest. They are easily taken for granted, for they don't need a lot of fussing and tending once in the ground. A bit of weeding now and then and an occasional pruning are all that are required, really.

We often put our herbs in the most neglected part of the yard, knowing that they'll do fine even if the soil is poor. Still, in no time at all, they are lush and big and ready to harvest. There are not a lot of plants that will sustain the abuse that herbs will and continue to produce with such vigor. They truly are special plants.

I had played around with growing herbs for several years when I had the chance to take a college course in England. I can still remember seeing the Queen's garden at Kew Garden, just outside London. The herbs were beautiful, the gardens charming and I think I knew even then that herbs were something really special to me and that I wanted to learn everything I could about them.

I started planting more and different herbs each year. I sought out new herbs to add each season, adding them to the old favorites from before. I was rarely disappointed. I was also hooked. For me, all other types of gardening would take a back seat to herbs. I lived on an herb farm for a time and designed a teaching garden on herbs at the Extension office where I was employed.

I had been teaching herb gardening for a while at that point, but I realized that what needed to be learned could not be covered in a two-hour lecture. That is how this book came about. On the advice of Dr. Peter Gail, I put down on paper what I knew of herbs from my own experiences. I wanted to share with others the joy of growing herbs. I wanted others to fall under their spell and to know their charm.

That is really what this book is about. Getting you started on the road to knowing and loving herbs as I do. This is no coffee table book to be displayed, but rather a workbook to come along with you and guide you on the journey to get your garden started and to enjoy the harvest.

Judi Strauss

http://www.TheCharmedKitchen.com

Revised January 2013

Table of Contents

Preface	7
Introduction	11
Choosing Your Site	13
Preparing Your Site	15
Planning Your Garden	17
Herb Listing	23
Starting Seeds Indoors	51
Propagation	55
Planting and Transplanting	57
Maintenance	59
Harvest and Storage	61
Plant and Seed Resource List	63
About the Author	71

Introduction

In recent years there has been a renewed interest in growing herbs. There are probably several reasons for this. Herbs are easy to grow and don't need a lot of TLC. For many of us, garden space is all too limited and herbs can be grown in small yards, among other landscape plants and flowers, and even in containers.

While most herbs need full sun, they are less fussy about the soil in which they are grown. With the wide variety of foliage shapes, sizes, and colors, herbs are also a beautiful addition to any yard. For most plants this would be more than enough, but with herbs this is only the beginning of the story. Herbs are not only lovely, low-maintenance additions to our lives, they are also useful. Herbs can flavor our food, fragrance our lives, color our clothes, and heal our bodies.

It is certainly no wonder that more people are growing herbs than ever before. Herbs have been an important part of our lives since earliest known history. Herbs and spices were used as money in some ancient civilizations. Much of the reason for interactions between ancient peoples was to trade for or even steal prized herbs and spices. While most herbs are reasonably priced, today you have only to price a gram of saffron to know that some herbs are worth their weight in gold.

In earlier days the study of medicine and botany were closely related. Plants were the only medicines that people had. Today we certainly could not imagine medical students referring to their herbal or discussing the benefits of peppermint or mullein. Still, even a few years ago we could not imagine finding herbal remedies at the corner drug store, either. You must be an informed consumer when it comes to herbal remedies. Some claims are unfounded or exaggerated. There is plenty of good, scientific research out there. Use it before deciding to take any herbal remedy. Herbs like comfrey, tansy, pennyroyal, sassafras, lobelia and wormwood are among the herbs that you should not be consuming in any form.

Still, most herbs are perfectly safe and many are beneficial at some level. Parsley contains large amounts of Vitamin C; mint teas can be soothing to the digestion; and the gel-like sap of the Aloe Vera plant can soothe the pain of minor burns. If cooking with herbs helps you to reduce the amount of sodium in your diet, the word "medicinal" could certainly be applied to any herb.

Whatever your reason for starting an herb garden, you can be sure of several things: Herbs will give you years of pleasure for a minimum of work. They will thrive where other plants have failed and herbs will add a touch of beauty and grace wherever they happen to grow. They are the workhorses of the garden, giving so much reward with so little effort. In a day when time is often the rarest of commodities, how lucky to have a garden that requires so little precious time.

Don't forget to follow my blog online at: http://www.TheCharmedKitchen.com.

Choosing Your Site

As in real estate, the three most important words to remember when growing herbs are location, location, and location. While herbs aren't as picky about their environment as some other plants, they do have some requirements for optimum growth.

Most of the herbs we grow today are native to the Mediterranean. They like the soil well-drained and they need plenty of sunlight. So, when picking out the place for your herb garden choose a location that is on high ground and receives full sun. This location should also fit into the overall landscape plan of your yard. For convenient harvesting, keep the herbs close to the house, if you can. That way you'll be more inclined to pick a sprig of this or that when making dinner.

To insure that your herb garden gets enough drainage, you can do several things. When choosing your location, avoid low spots in your yard. Also avoid any areas that seem to stay wet even several days after the last rainfall. Clay soils tend to hold water so if you have heavy clay soil plan on incorporating some sort of organic matter into the soil. Organic matter will help the soil to drain, and lessen its tendency to compact. You could use compost, leaf humus, peat moss, or well-rotted manure. Soil improvement will be discussed in more detail in the next chapter.

Another way to keep your herbs well drained is to use raised beds. Adding 6-10" of height to your garden will help the water to drain away from the roots of the herb plants. You can raise your garden bed through the addition of soil and organic matter to your site or you can simply rake excess soil from the pathways and edges to make the garden higher.

Many people like to enclose their raised bed gardens with a permanent border. Railroad ties are frequently used, but you can also use boards, bricks, stone, commercial edging or just about anything that will contain your soil. An added bonus in using a permanent border is that these structures help to contain herbs that have invasive growth habits, such as the mints. However, do not use any material that has been treated with dangerous chemicals, or that is not EPA approved for that purpose. Railroad ties are sometimes treated with creosote and pressure-treated lumber is treated with arsenic.

If your garden is already in the ground, but you feel that you need to improve drainage, you may not need to rip out everything and start over. Digging trenches around the perimeter of the garden will improve drainage. You can also add drainage tiles around an existing garden. Keep in mind, however, that if your soil is really heavy or your location really low these measures may not be enough. Sometimes a raised bed is the best solution to overcome existing environmental problems. As long as your herbs are in a reasonably well drained area they should do just fine.

Like vegetables, most herbs require full sun to be happy and healthy. There are a few herbs that will tolerate some shade, and a few that even require it, but these are clearly the exceptions. What does full sun mean? Generally, full sun means at least six hours of sunlight per day. Eight or more hours are even better.

Watch your yard to see where the sun shines the longest. Southern and western exposures are the sunniest, but buildings and trees will effect the total hours of sun that any area receives. If your yard is mostly shady, you might want to plant the herbs in containers that can be moved to receive the sunlight that they need.

If you have to choose between one location that is dry but shady, or one that is sunny and wet, choose the sunny spot. You can always raise the soil level. Don't get discouraged if no place seems quite perfect. Very few of us are fortunate enough to have ideal conditions for our gardens. Do the best you can with what you have, and remember: while herbs will thrive under ideal conditions they can still perform fairly well in less than perfect surroundings.

Preparing Your Site

Before you can plant your herb garden you will have to prepare the soil. This is done in several steps. First, the garden will have to be cleared of any unwanted plants. Mark off the area that you'll be using. You might also want to have the soil tested to find out what nutrients your garden may need. A soil test kit can be acquired through your local Extension office.

If the garden is to be planted where grass is growing, the sod will have to be pulled up. You can do one of two things with the grass that you remove. It can be placed root side up in a corner of the yard, covered with a thin layer of soil and allowed to decompose. Once completely broken down, this compost can be used in your herb garden or in flower and vegetable gardens as well. If you already have a compost pile add the grass to it instead.

If you don't mind the extra work the grass can be composted in the garden site itself. After the grass has been removed you'll have to dig out the soil in your garden to a depth of about 12". The grass is then placed in the dug out site, root side up, and the soil is replaced. The entire garden does not have to be dug out at once. You can also remove the soil in a series of trenches. Once your garden site is marked off and free of grass, the soil will have to be broken up in some way. Simply turning over the soil with a shovel and breaking up the big pieces will work well for a small garden. In a larger site you may wish to use a rototiller.

If organic matter needs to be added to the soil (and it probably does) add it to a depth of 2-6" over the entire garden. Organic matter like compost, well-rotted manure, leaf humus or peat moss should be spread over bare soil before it is cultivated. Then work the organic matter into the top 8-10 inches of soil. You might also want to add lime to your soil at this time. The only way to know for sure if you need lime is to have the soil tested. Lime is generally added at a rate of 2 pounds per 100 square feet. Because of the ability of herbs to thrive in poor soil you do not need to add fertilizer. Some herbs will be less flavorful if grown in highly fertile soil.

Because herbs do well in poor soils does not mean that you can skip the addition of organic matter. While they do not need highly fertile soil, many of the herbs that you will be growing will undoubtedly be perennials, and these plants will be growing in the same spot, undisturbed, for many years. It is crucial to give them a good start and a happy home. There is an old gardening adage that says that for every dollar you spend above the ground you should spend two below. It is too true. You must create a healthy garden bed to have a healthy garden.

It is also important to be sure, before you begin preparing your garden, that the soil is not too wet. Soil cultivated when too wet will clump together and dry into a horrible mess. To determine if your soil is dry enough to be worked, pick up a handful of soil and squeeze it in the palm of your hand. With the soil still in your palm, try to break it apart with your thumb. If it falls apart, the soil is ready to be turned and tilled.

It is widely believed that a cure for heavy clay soil is the addition of sand. This is just not true. If you add sand alone to clay soil you will end up with cement. Sand can be added in conjunction with organic matter, but if organic matter is being added you don't need sand.

While it may seem like a lot of work to prepare your soil, don't cut corners! Preparing the soil the right way will pay off for years to come. A well-prepared garden will all but ensure success for you and your plants.

Planning Your Garden

Before you begin planting your herb garden it is important to have a plan on paper. There are a number of factors to consider when getting your plan together. What you will eventually decide to plant depends on your likes and dislikes, the amount of room that you have, the amount of some herbs you'll want to harvest, your time, resources and needs. You may well change your plan several times before you actually start planting. Remember it is easier to change a plan on paper than it is to change it once planting is underway. Even the most experienced gardener is likely to change his or her plan several times before they arrive at a plan that best suits their needs.

To start, make a list of the herbs you would most like to grow. The next chapter is a listing of herbs with information on their soil and light requirements, as well as growth habits and uses. Refer to this list to help you decide. Consider the herbs that you use the most. A word of caution: Don't get too ambitious your first year. Keep your plan simple and workable. Better to have a small success than a big failure.

Try to keep your list down to 10-12 herbs to start. You can add new herbs to your garden from year to year. Some easy-to-grow herbs you may wish to include on your list are: basil, chives, dill, lavender, marjoram, oregano, parsley, lemon balm, tarragon, thyme, sage, savory, mints, cilantro, chervil and lovage. There are certainly others that you may wish to include. This list only intends to give you a starting point.

Once you have a list of what you'd like to grow, consider the amount of space available to be sure you'll have room for all the herbs you've chosen. You'll want to plant more of some herbs than others. One sage plant is probably more than enough for most families. Herbs like parsley, dill, basil, and cilantro are usually needed in larger quantities. Consider, too, if you'll want an extra amount of some herbs to freeze or dry for later use. If you determine that you have enough room for all the herbs on your list, you're one step closer to putting a plan on paper.

There are still some things you'll need to know before you draw up your plan. You'll have to know how tall the herb will grow. Taller herbs should be planted to the east or north side of the garden, so they won't shade lower growing plants. Also, find out how much the herb tends to spread from year to year. Mints, for example, are wonderful, versatile plants. However, they do send out lots of underground runners and can easily overtake a garden. If at all possible, keep mints in a separate part of your garden, or plant them in containers (above or in the ground) to keep them from spreading. If you choose to sink a container into the ground it must be bottomless, so water can drain sufficiently. The container should be set at least 12" into the ground and 1-2" above the soil line. Drain tiles can be used, as well as old coffee cans, flowerpots, or even old wastebaskets. Just be sure to remove the bottom. These containers are not foolproof, however. Sometimes mints planted in tiles can still escape, so be careful.

Be sure to find out, also, if the herbs that you are planting are annuals, biennials, or perennials. It's a good idea to keep annuals and biennials separate from perennials. Most perennials don't like to have their roots disturbed. By keeping the perennials together, you won't have to cultivate around them each year when you replant the annuals and some of the biennials.

Think about the type of garden you want to plant. Herb gardens can be formal or informal. Formal designs can be quite intricate, including knot designs, formal edgings, and geometric patterns. A formal design must be meticulously planned, planted, and maintained, to look good. Spacing of the plants must be exact, and they need to be pruned and weeded frequently. While a formal herb garden can be a stunning focal point in any yard they are time consuming and require a certain amount of expertise. If you are a beginner to the world of herb gardening, or just don't have the time, avoid a formal herb garden design.

The easier plan is certainly an informal one. It is also the type most widely planted. Herbs are planted alone or in groups throughout the garden. A low maintenance border or edging could be included in this plan. Some good edging plants include thyme, chives, germander, dwarf lavender, parsley and bush basil.

Flowers are traditionally included in herb gardens, and you may wish to do the same. Some flowers frequently included are: Dianthus, coreopsis, violets, marigolds, pansies, delphiniums, dusty miller, foxglove, nasturtiums, poppies, and roses. You may include any flower that you like, but be sure to use them as accents to the herb plants. If you add too many flowers the impact of the herbs may be lessened. However, since most herbs do not produce showy blooms, the addition of a few flowers can add a welcome splash of color.

When considering color in the herb garden don't overlook the varying shades of herbal foliage. Plants can vary from bright green to gray, blue, white, silver, purple or yellowish green. Give some thought as to how these different foliar hues will group together. You may wish to make a particularly striking plant the focal point of your garden.

With all the factors that must be considered when planning a garden you can see why good advice to the novice is: keep it simple. For a first garden, keep your list of herbs short and your plan informal. As you become more familiar with different herbs, you can gradually change and improve your plan with time.

When you put your plan on paper, keep the drawing to scale. Mark "North" on the plan and include a notation of any existing structures, such as buildings and fences. Also mark down any trees in the immediate area. With careful thought and planning you should be able to stick to what you eventually put down on paper.

Planning the garden may seem a bit overwhelming, but the extra care will show in your garden. A well-planned garden will require fewer changes over time, and will look good from the start. You'll also have the satisfaction of having a garden that reflects your own personal style and taste.

Even the best-planned garden will change over time. If you don't like your plan once it's planted, you should make notes of what you did and did not like, for changes next season. You will also certainly change what you are planting from year to year, and so each year your garden will differ. That is really part of the fun.

Herb Listing

This chapter contains a listing of 50 different herbs that you can grow. Information in this list includes sunlight requirements, life cycles, height, and methods of propagation and uses.

While this is not a listing of every herb you could ever grow, this should give you plenty of choices. I try to grow at least a couple of new herbs each year. There is no substitute for the experience of growing the herbs yourself to really appreciate their beauty and fragrance. It is also fun to keep a little room in your garden each season for a few "experiments". You may just find a new favorite among them.

The letter after each plant signifies the life cycle of that herb. The key is as follows:

A - Annual

A plant that completes its life cycle in a single season. These will need to be replanted each year, although some will re-seed.

B - Biennial

A plant that completes its life cycle in two years. Biennials produce only leaves their first season, and flower and die the second season. Sometimes, if the winter is mild, biennials will last to a third season.

P - Perennial

Any plant that lasts for more than two years. Depending on the plant, you can expect it to grow from three or four years up to twenty or more. Perennials are generally considered to be winter hardy, although in severe winters there will undoubtedly be plant losses.

TP - Tender Perennial

A plant that will live for more than two years if given protection from cold weather. This could include mulching the plant heavily during cold winter months, or better yet, bringing the plant indoors for the winter.

PP - Pot Plant

A plant that is best grown as a houseplant or in a container. Pot plants can often be put outdoors in milder weather and then brought back in before temperatures fall.

Index of Herbs

1. Aloe Vera
2. Angelica
3. Anise
4. Basil
5. Bay
6. Bergamot
7. Borage
8. Caraway
9. Catnip
10. Chamomile
11. Chervil
12. Chives
13. Cilantro
14. Cumin
15. Dill
16. Elecampane
17. Fennel
18. Fenugreek
19. Garlic Chives
20. Germander
21. Horehound
22. Hyssop
23. Lavender
24. Lemon Balm
25. Lemon Verbena
26. Lovage
27. Marjoram
28. Mint
29. Nasturtium
30. Oregano
31. Parsley
32. Pennyroyal
33. Pineapple Sage
34. Rocambole
35. Rosemary
36. Rue
37. Saffron
38. Sage
39. Salad Burnet
40. Santolina
41. Scented Geraniums
42. Sesame
43. Sorrel
44. Southernwood
45. Summer Savory
46. Sweet Cicely
47. Sweet Woodruff
48. Tarragon
49. Thyme
50. Winter Savory

1. ALOE (PP)

Aloe or Aloe Vera is also known as the first-aid plant for the healing properties of its gel-like sap. As a houseplant it will grow to a height of about 12". It is best propagated from the side shoots that develop around the base of the mother plant. These can simply be removed and replanted. Aloe prefers bright, indirect light. In a semi-shady area of your yard, aloe can be planted after all danger of frost is past, but it must be brought indoors for the winter.

2. ANGELICA (B)

Angelica is a large plant with deeply indented leaves. In its second or third year it sends up a flower stalk that can reach a height of 6 feet. While Angelica is propagated by seed, it is slow to germinate, and a purchased plant is probably the easiest solution. Angelica has a deep taproot, and thus should only be transplanted when the plant is less than 4" in height. Angelica prefers a semi-shady location and moist soil. It is a showy plant and can serve as a focal point. The stems are edible when boiled in sugar water and candied. Angelica is also used as a flavoring in some liqueurs.

3. ANISE (A)

Anise is a delicate plant that reaches a height of 2' when in bloom. It requires full sun and well-drained soil. Anise is easily started from seed. It does not like to be transplanted, and should be sown where it is to grow after all danger of frost is past. It can also be started in peat pots indoors and transplanted later, taking care not to disturb the roots. The seeds are used as a licorice flavoring in foods. Note: this is not Star Anise.

4. BASIL (A)

One of the most popular herbs in home gardens, basil is easily started from seed. It can be sown directly into the garden, or started indoors for a head start on the season. Basil likes full sun and well-drained soil. It should only be planted outdoors after all danger of frost has passed. Most basil grows to a height of 18-24". There are a number of cultivars available to you and all of them are worth a try. The most widely known is common or sweet basil. You can also grow basil with green ruffled leaves, purple leaves, purple ruffled leaves and bush or spicy globe basil with miniature leaves and a ball shaped plant. There is a lettuce or large leaved basil that can be used as you would grape leaves. There are also basils with scented leaves, including cinnamon, lemon, licorice, and holy basil with clove-scented foliage. The scented varieties are a little shorter than the other varieties. Basil leaves are used in tomato and meat dishes, as well as in Italian dishes, and basil is the main ingredient in pesto sauce. The basil blossoms can be used to flavor vinegars.

5. BAY (TP)

Bay is also known as Sweet Bay, or Bay Laurel. In mild climates it can be grown outdoors year round and can reach a height of 30' or more. Where there are hard frosts, however, Bay must be grown as a pot plant and brought indoors for winter. This plant should not be confused with Mountain Laurel, which is poisonous. Bay requires full sun and well-drained soil. It is best propagated from cuttings and may take several months to root, even if conditions are ideal. The purchase of a plant will save time and aggravation. Bay leaves can be used fresh or dried in soups and stews. It can also be used in wreaths and dried arrangements.

6. BERGAMOT (P)

Bergamot is also known as Bee Balm, Monarda, and Oswego Tea. This member of the mint family can grow to a height of 3'. Its flowers can be white, red, pink, maroon, or lavender. Most common are the reds and pinks. The blossoms are very sweet smelling, and as the name Bee Balm implies, they are very attractive to bees. The herb is also very attractive to hummingbirds. Bergamot will tolerate partial shade, but the plants will grow larger in full sun. Monarda also prefers moist soil. It can be started from seed. Established plants send out runners that can be separated from the mother plant and transplanted. The flowers are tasty and look pretty added to a salad. The leaves can be dried and used alone or with other herbs for a delightful tea, and can also be combined with flower petals in potpourri.

7. BORAGE (A)

Borage is a fast-growing herb that can easily be started from seed. It has a tendency to re-seed itself, so once borage is established in the garden you will usually not have to replant it for years to come. Borage forms a taproot early and should be sown where it is to grow. Borage can grow to a height of 2-3'. Its hairy leaves have a cucumber-like flavor and can be eaten raw in salads. It needs full sun and prefers somewhat dry soil. It has distinctive blue, star-shaped flowers that are also edible. Many people grow borage just for its flowers.

8. CARAWAY (B)

The leaves of caraway resemble shiny carrot leaves. During the first year the plant only grows to a height of 6", but the following season it sends up a beautiful flower spike that will reach a height of 2'. Caraway has a tap root and so should be sown where it is to grow. Caraway needs full sun and good drainage. This herb is grown for its flavorful seeds, which are used in rye bread, potato, cabbage, and carrot dishes, as well as to flavor the liqueur Akavit.

9. CATNIP (P)

Catnip is easily started from seed, and should be part of your garden if a feline is part of your life. A word of warning: catnip will also attract neighborhood kitties to your yard to roll and frolic about in it. The plant has heart-shaped grayish leaves. When not in flower it has a rather compact growth habit at about 1' in height. In flower it sends up flower stalks to a height of up to 3', and becomes a little unruly in appearance. Catnip will thrive in full sun and well drained soil. Catnip is grown to be enjoyed by cats, either fresh or dried. Many humans enjoy it as an herb tea. It is also said to repel flea beetles.

10. CHAMOMILE (P/A)

There are 2 types of chamomile grown in home gardens. German chamomile is an annual; Roman chamomile is a perennial. Both are grown for their daisy-like flowers, used to make tea. Both require full sun for best flower production and both will tolerate moist soil.

German chamomile grows to a height of 2-2 1/2 ' when in flower. It forms a taproot early and should be started from seed where it is to grow. If some flowers are left on the plant it does tend to re-seed itself. German chamomile flowers have a pleasant apple flavor.

Roman chamomile grows in a dense, 6" feathery mass, sending up flowers heads to a height of 12-18". Like German Chamomile, it can be started from seed. It also sends out long side roots, which make it hard to move later on. The tea from the Roman variety is less sweet than its annual counterpart. The dried blossoms of Roman chamomile, when steeped in warm water are said to make a nice hair rinse for blondes. A word of caution: if you are allergic to ragweed you should avoid consuming chamomile tea.

11. CHERVIL (A)

Though considered an annual, chervil is more properly called a hardy annual. This means that it can overwinter if the seeds are sown in the late summer. Chervil looks like parsley, but the leaves are more delicate and a lighter green. Chervil is best grown in partial shade as it quickly goes to seed and dies when the weather is hot and dry. The leaves taste a little like French tarragon, and chervil is sometimes used as a substitute. Chervil will not hold its flavor when dried, and so should be used fresh, or frozen for later use. Chervil grows to a height of 10", and can reach a height of 2' when in flower. Unlike many herbs, chervil likes its soil rich and moist for best growth. Chervil also does well as a houseplant, and if sown in pots in late August, will provide you with fresh leaves throughout the winter. Chervil is wonderful in omelets and any vegetable dish.

12. CHIVES (P)

This hardy plant is a welcome and useful addition to any herb garden. It is grown for its tender, mild, onion-flavored foliage chives also produce an abundance of pretty purple flowers that are useful. Chives require full sun for best growth and prefer the soil well drained. It can be started easily from seed, started indoors, or sown directly in the garden. An established clump can also be dug up and divided as a means of propagation.

Chives will grow to a height of about 12", but this varies, as there are several varieties available. The leaves are used fresh, frozen, and dried in a variety of dishes including meat, poultry and vegetables. The blossoms are edible and can be added to salads or used to flavor vinegars. They can also be dried and used in winter floral arrangements. See also: GARLIC CHIVES.

13. CILANTRO (A)

Cilantro, known as coriander and Chinese parsley, is easy to grow from seed and should be planted where it is to grow. Cilantro needs to be planted as early in the spring as the ground can be worked since it goes to seed quickly once the weather gets hot. The leaves of cilantro resemble lacy parsley, and will reach a height of about 12". The leaves and seeds are both edible. Latino cooking most often uses the leaves, while Asian cuisine more commonly uses the seeds. When referring to the seeds, cilantro is usually called coriander. Cilantro leaves are essential in the Hispanic dish sofrito. The leaves are also used in some Far East cuisines. The taste is rather pungent, but pleasant and different from any other herb.

Cilantro requires full sun and well-drained soil for best performance. Because of cilantro's dislike for midsummer heat it is best grown as a spring or fall crop.

14. CUMIN (A)

This tiny member of the parsley family should be grown for the novelty, rather than in the hope of measurable seed production. The seeds are what Cumin is grown for, but this plant needs 4 months of hot weather to set seed. You can start Cumin indoors 6 weeks before setting it out in late spring or early summer. The seeds need temperatures of 70-75 degrees to germinate. The roots are tender and must be handled carefully when transplanting. Cumin requires full sun and plenty of heat to do well. It will not exceed 12" in height. The plants have a very feathery appearance and should be grown close together to lend support to each other, as they tend to fall over in rainstorms. The crushed seeds are used in chili powder and curry dishes.

15. DILL (A)

Dill is a must if you are also growing cucumbers for homemade pickles. On appearance alone, dill is a welcome addition to any garden. It is a feathery, delicate looking plant that can reach a height of 3'. When dill gets tall it should be given some support to keep it from falling over in high winds. If you plant your dill in a clump, rather than in rows, you can put a few stakes around the plants, and run twine around it for support. Dill does not transplant well, and seed should be sown where it is to grow. Dill is tolerant of cold and can be planted early in the spring. It requires full sun and well-drained soil. While both the leaves and seeds are edible, some types of dill go to seed rather quickly, making the leaves less tasty. A variety of dill, called Dukat, does not grow as tall as most types, and delays flowering by several weeks over other cultivars.

Dill seed heads are used in pickle making. The mature seeds are used in salad dressings and potato salads. The dill leaves or weed) are used in carrot, potato, and other vegetable dishes.

16. ELECAMPANE (P)

Elecampane is a shrubby perennial that can grow to a height of 4-6'. It has long, narrow leaves and produces lovely, sunflower-like blooms. It needs full sun and moist soil for best growth. Elecampane makes a nice background plant in herb gardens. It can be propagated from root divisions or from seeds, but it will not flower the first year when started from seed. Elecampane is also called horseheal, because the roots, when ground up and mixed with lard, were used as a horse liniment. In the past the bitter roots were also dried and steeped to make a tea with reported healing properties. These claims are unproven, however, and today Elecampane is grown only as an ornamental.

17. FENNEL (P)

Fennel resembles dill in appearance, although once you've crushed a few leaves, there will be no trouble in telling them apart. Fennel has a pungent, anise-like flavor. Fennel requires full sun for best results. It also will not tolerate wet soils; in fact, soil that is too wet will cause fennel to die over winter. It is easily started from seed, which is best sown where the fennel is to grow. It can grow to a height of 4-5'.

The other variety of fennel you may wish to grow is Florence fennel, which forms a swollen stem at the base. This stem is eaten raw in salads and relish trays. Florence fennel is dug up for its stems, and so should be thought of as an annual.

There is also an ornamental variety called Bronze fennel, which is grown for its lovely foliage. As with dill, both the fennel seeds and leaves are used. The leaves can be used for herb tea, or can be placed on the coals to enhance the flavor of grilled foods, especially fish. The seeds are sometimes used in rye breads and cookies, and are an essential ingredient in Italian sausage.

18. FENUGREEK (A)

This tiny member of the legume family produces pink flowers on 2' tall stalks. It requires full sun and very good drainage to flourish. Fenugreek should be started from seed once the soil is warm. The seed should be sown where it is to grow. The seeds, which will form in brown pods, are used for their maple flavor. The leaves also have a slight maple flavor, but it is in the seed where the flavor is strongest. The seeds can be ground up and added to cakes and cookies for maple flavoring. They are also boiled in sugar syrup as a topping for pancakes. Fenugreek is one of the herbs used in curry powder.

19. GARLIC CHIVES (P)

Like their relative, chives, garlic chives are hardy plants that will naturally grow in clumps. Unlike chives, garlic chives have flat leaves, rather than hollow. They require full sun and well-drained soil. Garlic chives can be started from seed or by division of an established clump. They will not flower the first year from seed, but will flourish the second season. In fact, garlic chives thicken so quickly that you should be sure to keep first year clumps small. They have a pleasant garlic-onion flavor, and will produce a mass of lovely white flowers in August and September. Garlic chives do well as a pot plant. The leaves are used to flavor any food where you would use onion or garlic.

20. GERMANDER (P)

There are 2 types of germander available on the market. The Upright, or Wall germander, grows to a height of about 12". It is a pretty plant, whose compact growth habit makes it ideal for hedges and borders in formal herb gardens. Even in an informal plan, the use of germander as a border lends an air of structure to a garden. Upright germander will send up flower stalks with pretty pink blooms in midsummer. In a formal or knot garden you may wish to trim off these blooms to keep the germander looking well groomed. In a less formal setting, you may as well leave them on and enjoy their beauty.

The other germander is a low growing variety called prostrate germander. It has an invasive growth habit and can quickly become a nuisance plant.

While germander can be started from seed, it will not get very large the first year. Cuttings or divisions of established plants are the preferred methods of propagation. Germander will tolerate partial shade, but will become fuller and bushier in full sun. It also requires well drained soil. In areas with hard winters, some winter protection is also recommended. This can be accomplished with leaves or branches placed over germander during the winter months to keep it green. Germander's main use today is ornamental.

21. HOREHOUND (P)

There are 2 types of horehound found in nurseries and garden centers today. White horehound has a creeping habit and will not exceed 2' in height. Silver horehound is an upright and showier plant for the home garden. Both require full sun and good drainage. In both types, heavy clay soil may cause winterkill. Horehound can be started from seed and will even re-seed itself in subsequent years. The leaves are used to make herb tea, or boiled in sugar syrup to make a hard candy that is said to be soothing to the throat.

22. HYSSOP (P)

Hyssop is an attractive plant that will grow to a height of 2'. It works well as a border or edging plant. If you prefer the less groomed look, you can allow it to flower, rather than trimming it. The flowers of hyssop may be deep blue, pink, or white. Hyssop need full sun for best growth, but will tolerate partial shade. It can be started from seed, and new plants should be set in the garden about 12" apart. The plants will be small the first year, but will spread out the second.

Hyssop's only known use is as an ornamental. The foliage, while attractive, has a "skunky", musky sort of smell.

23. LAVENDER (P/A)

There are 2 main types of lavender you can grow in your garden. English lavender is a perennial; in northern climates, French lavender is an annual. Both require full sun and good drainage. Both can be started from seed, although English lavender is slow to germinate and can be a little tricky. Both types can also be started from cuttings and layering. There are many varieties of both lavenders, although some may be difficult to find. An English lavender variety you may wish to try is Munstead, which grows to a height of 2' and bears true lavender-colored flowers. Other varieties include Hidcote, with dark purple spikes; Alba, with white blooms; Jean Davis, with pink flowers; and Dutch with deep blue flowers. All are wonderfully scented. The foliage of French lavenders is greener than that of English types.

Lavender grows quickly once it is established, and can get quite tall in mild climates. French lavender can also be grown as a houseplant during cold winter months, and moved outdoors during the summer.

Lavenders are grown for their intoxicating fragrance. Some say that the smell of lavender can reduce headaches. The flowers are harvested just as they begin to open, and are dried on the stalk. These dried blooms can then be used in arrangements, or the blooms can be stripped from the stem and used in potpourri and sachet.

24. LEMON BALM (P)

Lemon balm forms thick clumps, of dark green, heart-shaped leaves, 2-3' tall. It is available in a yellow and green variegated cultivar. Although it is a member of the mint family, lemon balm does not send out underground runners like other mints. It will re-seed itself in abundance. If you don't want thousands of new lemon balm plants, keeping the flowers trimmed off as they appear will prevent seed production.

Lemon balm starts easily from seed. It thrives in full sun but will tolerate partial shade. Good drainage is critical, as lemon balm may die off over winter in heavy, wet soils.

Lemon balm is grown for its strongly lemon-scented leaves. But, while the fragrance is strong, the leaves do not impart a strong lemon flavor. They are best used fresh or with other herbs in a tea blend. Lemon balm leaves are also a nice addition to sachet and potpourri.

25. LEMON VERBENA (TP/PP)

In warm climates, lemon verbena can grow to a height of 10-12'. In colder climates this just doesn't happen, although the plant can grow 2-3' in a single season. The leaves give off a delightful lemon scent when they are touched. Lemon verbena can be brought in for the winter, but it needs a dormant period to spur fresh growth, as well as full sun and well-drained soil for best results. Lemon verbena is best propagated from cuttings.

The leaves give a lemon flavor to foods, but should be removed before serving as they are very chewy. The leaves are also used in herb teas and potpourri.

26. LOVAGE (P)

Lovage is sometimes called the celery plant and for very good reason. It looks a lot like celery; the leaves and seeds taste like celery; and both plants need the same conditions for best growth. Lovage needs full sun and rich, moist soil in order to perform well in your garden. It can easily be started from seed and can handle transplanting. A healthy lovage plant can grow into a 2' wide clump quickly. It will reach a height of about 3' when not in bloom. When flowering, lovage sends up seed heads that can reach a height of 6'. Lovage leaves can be used as a substitute for celery leaves in flavoring soups and stews. The seeds can also be used as a substitute for celery seeds in cooking, but have a stronger flavor than celery seed.

27. MARJORAM (TP)

Sweet marjoram is sometimes mistaken for oregano by the home gardener. The two herbs have similar leaves and are closely related botanicals. While sweet marjoram is grown as an annual throughout most of the country, oregano is a hardy perennial. The flavor and fragrance are also different. Marjoram's flavor is sweeter and more subtle than oregano.

Marjoram can be started from seed, but the seedlings are prone to damping off disease. Take care not to over water them use only sterile potting mix and allow good air circulation around young seedlings. You can also sow the seeds directly in the ground where they are to grow, after all danger of frost is past.

Pot marjoram, a close relative, can be grown as a tender perennial or as the pot plant the name suggests. For best growth marjoram needs full sun and good drainage. The leaves will stay green well into winter, but freezing damages its roots. Some gardeners report marjoram overwintering, but they may be growing wild marjoram, or even a type of oregano.

Marjoram has a spreading growth habit and can reach a height of about 18" in northern gardens. Marjoram leaves are used to flavor meat dishes, especially beef. They also add flavor to salad dressings, and can be used to flavor vinegars.

28. MINT (P)

When the word "mint" is said, most people think of common mint, or perhaps peppermint and spearmint. In truth, there are dozens of plants with different appearances, flavors and fragrances and all are mints. Don't limit your garden choices to the more common types! These other varieties offer diversity well worth trying in your herb garden. All mints grow both in full sun and partial shade. Varieties with variegated leaves will maintain more color in their leaves when grown in some shade. Another thing all true mints have in common is their penchant for sending out underground runners, an invasive quality that can soon create problems if left unchecked. To contain the mints, you can plant them in bottomless containers (to insure good drainage) sunk in the ground to reduce runners. This is not a perfect solution, however. Some mints react poorly to this confinement, and will eventually die. A landscape planter such as a half wine barrel may be a better answer. You can also plant your mint in a separate area of the garden, surrounded by grass from the rest of the garden.

Mints can be started from seed, either directly in the garden or indoors ahead of time. The height of mints varies from the less than 6" of the Corsican mint to the 3' height of both Spearmint and Apple mint. Some of the other varieties include Pineapple mint, Austrian mint, Peppermint, Orange mint and Curled mint. Mint leaves are used to make teas, to flavor meats and vegetable dishes, and in potpourri. When planted close together, mints will cross pollinate, creating generally inferior hybrids. Keep mint flowers trimmed off to prevent this, or pull out seedlings as they appear.

29. NASTURTIUMS (A)

While considered by many to be merely flowers, nasturtiums are also herbs because their flowers and leaves can add real spice to our salad plate. Nasturtiums are a good substitute for watercress. They are easy to start from seed, and while they can be transplanted, nasturtiums will grow better when sown where they are to grow. These plants like full sun and can vary widely in height and growth habit depending on the variety you choose. There are types that grow upright and make nice edging plants, as well as cultivars that vine making them good hanging plants or fence climbers. Nasturtiums grow well in all but super wet conditions.

30. OREGANO (P)

This relative of marjoram is available in several varieties. While some of them are less hardy than others, with winter protection any type should survive sub-zero temperatures. Common oregano, or oregano vulgaris, is widely grown, but it is not the best culinary herb. It just doesn't have much flavor when fresh, and has even less when dried. And although common oregano is an attractive plant, it can be invasive. For your herb garden, grow either Greek or Mexican oregano. Both have the true "pizza" flavor that oregano is noted for.

Oregano needs full sun and dry soil to develop its best flavor. Different varieties vary in height from 1-2' and can be started from seed or from divisions of established plants. Commonly used in Italian cuisine and tomato dishes, oregano is also good in salad dressings and vinegars.

31. PARSLEY (B)

Parsley is certainly one of the most popular herbs grown in American gardens today. It is as popular in our kitchens as well. Parsley has a mild taste, which is goes well with many foods. It is also high in vitamin C. Parsley is started from seed which is slow to germinate, but easy to grow otherwise. It can be started indoors ahead of the season or sown directly in the garden. Parsley is fairly tolerant of light frost, and can be planted in late spring. It needs full sun and prefers well drained soil.

There are 3 types of parsley that you can grow including moss or curled parsley, flat or Italian parsley, and root or Hamburg parsley. The first 2 types are grown for their foliage. The third type is grown for its root, used to flavor soup stocks. While parsley is a biennial, it will quickly go to seed in its second season, making the leaves less tasty. Early in the spring of the second year, harvest the entire plant, before it goes to seed. Then you can replace the plant with a new one or re-seed the area. Parsley grows to a height of about 1'. It is used to flavor just about everything from meat and veggies to poultry and fish. It is used as a garnish because originally the parsley was nibbled at the end of the meal to freshen ones breath.

32. PENNYROYAL (P)

Pennyroyal is a member of the mint family with a low, creeping growth habit. In areas where grass will not grow, it is sometimes used as a lawn. In late summer it puts up 1' tall flower stalks. Pennyroyal can be grown in sun or shade, and will grow in soil that is wet or dry. It can easily be started from seed indoors or directly sown in the garden. Pennyroyal is sometimes used as a tea herb but there are some risks. Women of child- bearing years should not consume pennyroyal because it is said to induce abortion. A safer use of pennyroyal is as a natural insect repellent. To some, the smell of pennyroyal is similar to that of citronella.

33. PINEAPPLE SAGE (TP)

Pineapple sage is certainly one of the prettiest plants you can grow. It grows quickly into a bright green shrub that can reach a height of 3'. In late summer, pineapple sage sends up bright red flower spikes that will hold on for weeks. A delightful pineapple scent is released when the leaves are crushed. It will grow in full sun or partial shade, but needs dry soil to grow at its best. Pineapple sage is best propagated through cuttings. Although it will not survive cold winters, it can be brought indoors for the winter and replanted outdoors each spring. This way you can enjoy your plant for years. You can also start cuttings each fall and plant them outdoors in spring. The leaves are used to garnish fruit salads and can add a nice taste to marinades, especially for pork and chicken. The leaves can also be used fresh in flower arrangements, and dried in potpourri.

34. ROCAMBOLE (P)

Rocambole is a member of the onion or Allium family and is sometimes called French garlic. It grows in clumps, and has flat leaves that resemble both garlic and garlic chives. It will grow to a height of 18". Round stalks emerge from the center of the clump and will reach a height of 3'. These stalks produce popcorn-sized bulbets that have a mild garlic flavor. These little bulbs can be used in any dish requiring garlic. They also provide one means of propagation. The clump can also be dug up and divided for new plants. Rocambole likes full sun, but otherwise is not fussy. It will grow somewhat larger in rich, loamy soil.

35. ROSEMARY (TP)

Rosemary is an attractive, narrow-leaved shrub with a spicy aroma and graceful appearance. It is rather slow growing, and even a small plant is likely to be expensive. However, if brought indoors during cold weather, rosemary can last for years. In the garden, rosemary needs full sun and good drainage. Its leaves have a pine like scent, only sweeter. Some varieties can be started from seed, and all can be started from cuttings. Rosemary can be grown as a pot plant year round, or planted into the ground each spring and repotted in the fall. The leaves are used in cooking, traditionally with lamb and pork. It is also used as a tea herb, and makes a pleasant addition to sachets.

36. RUE (P)

The first thing you'll notice about rue is its striking blue-green foliage. The plant grows into a shrub that does not exceed 3' in height. It also produces yellow flowers that contrast nicely with the foliage. Because of its compact growth habit and dramatic color, rue is often used as a border plant. It needs full sun and will not overwinter in wet soil. Rue can be started from seed either indoors or directly in the ground. Mature foliage is a skin irritant. Rue's main use is an ornamental.

37. SAFFRON (P)

Saffron will certainly be the most valuable plant in your garden. Saffron threads are the stigmas gathered from the blooms of a fall-blooming crocus. There is very little yield from a single plant, and the gathering is tedious. Still, the plants are pretty enough to include them in your garden on looks alone. The stems grow about 3-4" tall and support a lavender, star-like flower. The leaves can reach a height of 5-6" and may stay green straight through until spring. Saffron is propagated through 1" corms that are planted in late summer. The corms multiply naturally underground, and can be divided every few years. Saffron will tolerate a bit of shade, but prefers full sun. It also prefers dry soil. The tiny threads are most often used in chicken and rice dishes.

38. SAGE (P)

Garden sage is an attractive plant that gets woody after its first year and resembles a small shrub. It will grow to a height of about 3'. Sage most often has purplish leaves, but is also found with yellow and green variegated leaves, as well as a tricolor cultivar. The more colorful varieties frequently lose their color after a cold winter and instead turn a bright green. Sage can easily be started from seed or from cuttings. It needs full sun and well-drained soil. Sage is used in poultry dishes and stuffing. It can also be used, alone or with other herbs, as tea.

39. SALAD BURNET (P)

Salad burnet is a member of the rose family, although their appearances are quite different. Salad burnet is a low growing plant that has dark green leaves with the scent and flavor of cucumber. It requires very well drained soil and, given the choice, will produce best in sandy soil. It also needs full sun. It is started from seed, and can be sown directly into the garden or started indoors and transplanted when small. Later on it develops a deep taproot that makes transplanting difficult. The leaves are used in salads for their cucumber taste, and to flavor vinegars.

40. SANTOLINA (P)

There are several types of santolinas grown in home gardens. The most popular of these is certainly Grey Santolina. It is also known as lavender cotton because of its soft, delicate appearance and delightful fragrance. All santolinas need full sun and light, well-drained soil. They grow to a height of 2-3', and are frequently used as border plants because of their compact growth habit and attractive appearance. Though santolinas can be started from seed, they are most successfully started from stem cuttings. When in flower, Grey Santolina produces yellow, button blooms several inches above the leaves. Santolinas dry well and are used in nosegays and tussie mussies. The fragrant leaves are also used in potpourri.

41. SCENTED GERANIUMS (A/PP)

When considering scented geraniums, forget any preconceived notions of what geraniums look like. Scented geraniums are grown for their fragrant leaves and interesting foliage. Most types produce uninteresting flowers. The number of scented geraniums available is quite large, and includes Rose, Lemon, Ginger, Chocolate, Lime, Pineapple, Apple, Apricot, Nutmeg and Mint. All can be started from seeds and cuttings. They prefer full sun and light soil. Scented geraniums are better adapted to pot culture than more traditional geraniums. They can do quite well as houseplants, even during the winter. Height of the plants varies from one type to the next, though most fall into the 18-24" range. The leaves are used in sachet and potpourri. Rose geranium leaves are also used in cooking as a flavoring in jelly and to make tea.

42. SESAME (A)

Sesame is a fast growing plant that needs plenty of sun and warmth for best growth. Sesame also does not like to be crowded and prefers moist soil. It will grow to a height of 3' in an ideal environment. Sesame is started from seed and can be started indoors, but must be transplanted when small, due to its taproot. Sesame produces lovely spikes of white flowers that will spit out their seeds if not harvested promptly. The seeds are used in cooking, and in the production of oil.

43. SORREL (P)

Sorrel is also known as French sorrel and garden sorrel. It's a member of the dock family and its less cultivated relatives can be harvested in most any field. The sorrel grown in herb gardens produces larger leaves, and is milder in flavor, than its wild cousins. French sorrel produces large, pointed leaves on 6" stems. When in flower, the plant sends up flower stalks that can reach more than 3' in height. Sorrel is started from seed, either indoors or directly sown in the garden. It needs full sun and well-drained soil. The leaves have a sour, almost lemony flavor that is used in dishes like sorrel soup. Young leaves can also be served raw in salads. To encourage new, tender growth sorrel can be cut back to the soil line.

44. SOUTHERNWOOD (P)

There are several types of southernwood available to home gardeners. The most common varieties are Lemon southernwood, and Camphor southernwood. Both of these Artemisias have thin leaves and woody stems. The lemon variety has a somewhat more compact growth habit. They grow to a height of 2-3', and need full sun and well-drained soil for best growth. Dried southernwood is sometimes strewn on a fire to sweeten the air, and the leaves are also used in potpourri. The camphor-scented variety is also used as an insect repellent. Both varieties can be propagated from stem cuttings.

45. SUMMER SAVORY (A)

Summer savory is an easy to grow herb that can be started from seed either directly sown in the garden, or started indoors. It will grow quickly to a height of 18". Summer savory needs full sun and well-drained soil for best growth. The leaves are narrow and dark green, and the plant produces pink flowers in late summer. Savory is sometimes called the "bean herb" because it is frequently used in bean dishes. Savory is also used in other vegetable dishes, and sometimes as a sage substitute in poultry stuffing. It has a tendency to re-seed itself, and these "volunteers" are often stronger than the seeds we sow each year.
See Also: WINTER SAVORY.

46. SWEET CICELY (P)

Sweet cicely is a fernlike plant that can grow to a height of 2' and resembles chervil. It prefers shade, and produces white flowers on tall stems in May that are quite showy. The leaves have an anise flavor and are used in cooking. Sweet cicely needs rich humus in which to grow. It is propagated from seed, which is slow to germinate. Seeds, which fall off the plant in August, can be left to insure extra Sweet Cicely in your yard. Because of its anise flavor Sweet cicely can be used as a substitute for fennel or French tarragon. Its leaves are sometimes broiled with fish.

47. SWEET WOODRUFF (P)

This shade-loving plant is a delight wherever it is grown. It is a sweet- smelling ground cover that will grow to a height of about 6", and is covered with a mass of white flowers every May. Woodruff can be grown in partial shade and will tolerate nearly full sun. It prefers moist soil, and rotted leaves should be incorporated into the soil before planting. Seeds are very slow to germinate, and you'd probably be better off purchasing a few plants. Woodruff will spread and can be divided every few years. The blossoms are used to flavor May wine. The leaves of sweet woodruff smell like new mown hay as they dry, and can be used as a natural room freshener. The leaves maintain their sweetness when dry making a nice addition to potpourri and sachet.

48. TARRAGON (P)

While you may see seeds for tarragon in a store or seed catalog from time to time, avoid them. True French tarragon never sets seeds, and can only be propagated from cuttings and root divisions. Tarragon started from seed is a poor culinary choice indeed. Tarragon is a narrow-leaved member of the Artemisia family that produces anise-flavored foliage. It will grow to a height of about 2'. Although tarragon is a hardy plant it may not survive winter if the soil is too wet. It also needs full sun to prosper. Tarragon is most often used in chicken and fish dishes, and to flavor vinegars.

49. THYME (P)

Common thyme is a creeping, evergreen plant with tiny green leaves, an ideal plant for edgings and rock gardens. There are other varieties of thyme, and all are edible. There is the attractive Lemon thyme, with its yellow and green leaves, as well as French thyme, with its gray, curling leaves. Other types include Silver thyme, Annie Hall, Mother of thyme, Wild thyme, Wooly thyme, and Oregano thyme. All thymes need full sun, and they will not survive in heavy, wet soil. Thyme can be started from seed, but is slow to germinate. Layering is the quickest method of propagation. Thymes generally grow to a height of 8-12", but there are whole groups that have a creeping habit and don't grow more than a few inches in height.

Thymes can be used fresh or dried in a variety of dishes, including beef, lamb, and pork. It has a strong flavor, and should be used with a light hand so as not to overpower a dish. The leaves of Lemon thyme can be added to potpourri. Thymes can also be used in herb teas.

50. WINTER SAVORY (P)

Winter savory is a compact plant with narrow green leaves that does not exceed 10" in height. It resembles a miniature shrub and makes a nice border plant in herb gardens. Winter savory requires full sun and well-drained soil. It can be started from seed indoors about 8 weeks before you want to set it in your garden. Like summer savory, winter savory is used in bean dishes. It can also be used in vegetable and chicken dishes and in poultry stuffing. See Also: SUMMER SAVORY.

Starting Seeds Indoors

To get a head start on the season you may decide to start some herbs indoors. Some herbs are difficult to start from seed, making a purchased plant an attractive option. Still, there are plenty of herbs that are easy to start from seed, and well worth the effort. Some of the easiest to start include basil, parsley, sweet marjoram, summer savory and fenugreek. Refer to the plant listing for information on specific herbs.

To insure success you will have to create the right environment. You'll need to provide your seeds with clean soil, moisture, light, correct temperature, good air circulation and nourishment.

The containers that you use must be clean and have holes for drainage. Plastic cell packs, such as nurseries use, are an inexpensive, reliable choice. They come in a multitude of sizes, and can be reused if they are cleaned thoroughly. You can also recycle things like egg cartons, milk cartons, margarine tubs and paper cups. Just make sure that whatever container you choose has drainage holes.

You will also need a sterile potting mix. Seed starting formulas are sometimes called "soilless" mixes because they are made up of several components, none of which are soil. These mixes are a combination of peat moss, perlite, vermiculite and sand. They are called "sterile" because they contain no weed seeds or bacteria found in garden soil. Soilless mixes are also lighter than plain soil, enabling roots to grow easily. The mix you use may or may not contain fertilizer. Check the bag. If the mix you are using contains no fertilizer, plan on watering seedlings with a plant food like Rapid-Gro or Peter's after they've sprouted.

Make sure that your seedlings have enough light. Inadequate light is probably the biggest mistake people make when starting seeds indoors. Poor light will result in spindly plants. A sunny window (west or south) will work, but don't allow seedlings to touch the glass. You can also use artificial light. Grow lights should be no more than 6" above the plants, and they must be on 14-16 hours per day. You can invest in a timer, turn them on and off manually or just leave them on all the time. Also, don't use regular fluorescent tubes. You must use wide spectrum lights (grow lights), or a combination of warm and cool fluorescent lights. Some seeds need light to germinate, and others may need to be in the dark. Check your seed packet.

Seeds also need different temperatures at which to germinate. Again, check the seed packet. For seeds requiring bottom heat, you may wish to invest in heating cables (available in many garden centers), or sprout your seeds on top of the fridge. Seeds requiring cool temperatures in which to germinate can be started in a basement. Invest in some plant markers, too, and a waterproof marking pen.

You can sow your seeds one of two ways. Seeds can be planted directly into the individual pots in which they will grow, or they can be sown in a larger pot (12-24 seeds), and transplanted to individual pots later. When sowing seeds directly into cell packs, plant 2 seeds per container. Cut off or remove the smaller of the 2 seedlings later. Since all seeds do not germinate, some cell packs will already contain only one plant.

If you decide to sow your seeds in pots and transplant them into cell packs later, they must be allowed to develop their second pair of leaves first. Remove them from the pot gently, using a small spoon or Popsicle stick to loosen the roots. Hold the plant by a leaf; the stems are very delicate and easily damaged. Set the plant in a cell pack, planting it a little deeper than it was growing. Firm the soil around the plant gently.

Whichever method you choose, always pre-moisten your soilless mix. They almost repel water at first. Set the trays or pots in 2-3" of warm water until the top of the soil feels damp. Depth of planting seeds differs from plant to plant. Generally, seeds are planted at a depth of 3x their diameter, but check the seed packet to be sure.

If seeds are allowed to dry out they won't sprout. To keep the soil moist, cover the pots with some clear covering to allow light in and keep in moisture. As soon as plants sprout the covering must be removed, to prevent molds from forming. Don't put any covering directly on top of the soil, or seeds will not be able to sprout. There are plastic domes available that fit cell pack trays perfectly.

Don't let cell packs or pots remain in standing water. Excess moisture may cause plants to rot. Plants also need good air circulation to prevent disease. Grow them in an open area, not in a closet or storage area.

Don't start seeds too early. Count back 6-8 weeks before the date you wish to plant your seedlings outside, and start them then. For very slow-growing herbs, you may have to start them as much as 12 weeks ahead of time. By now I'm feeling like a broken record, but, check the seed packet.

Seedlings will also need a time period in which to harden off. This just means setting them outside for a few hours a day about 10 days before transplanting them. Increase the time they are outside every day, and let them dry out a little between watering. This will toughen the plants, making transplanting a less stressful event. Provide them an area with some protection from full sun and strong winds for the first few days.

Starting seeds indoors does require some time and effort, but for herbs you will need in quantity, it is still worth the effort.

Propagation

In the listing of herbs, some different methods of propagation were mentioned. Seed starting has been described, but you may want to try other methods of propagating herb plants. The following descriptions should be of help to you.

Cuttings

When starting a plant from a stem cutting, you need to get a small piece of the herb. Usually a 2-3" piece will work best. Avoid using plants that are in flower. Strip off the lower leaves and dip the stem in water, then in rooting powder (Rootone). Now place the cutting in damp sand, perlite or vermiculite. Cover the cutting loosely with a small plastic bag and put it where it will receive filtered sunlight. Check the plant to make sure it does not dry out. When you start to see new growth, remove the plastic bag and move the plant to an area of greater light.

Root Divisions

A root division is simply a piece of plant root removed from the mother plant and potted up to start a new herb. As with the stem cutting, put the root in damp sand or vermiculite and cover with plastic until new growth appears.

Plant Divisions

Plant division involves digging up your herb plant and breaking or cutting it into 2 or more pieces. This should only be done when your plant is small (early spring).Try to leave as many of the roots intact as possible. You may also wish to cut off some of the leaves to give the root system less foliage to maintain while the plant recovers from the shock of division. If you want, you can wash the plant roots with the hose before dividing to make it easier to see what you are doing.

Layering

Many herbs will send out roots from any piece of stem that happens to be touching the ground. Thymes are a prime example. You can cut off and pot up any stem pieces that have done this on their own. You can also use a floral pick or even a clothespin to hold a piece of stem against the soil to start new root growth. Mounding some soil over the stem will encourage rooting. Once roots are formed, cut the stem piece away from the mother plant.

Corms, Bulbs, Cloves

These underground plant parts will naturally multiply during the growing season. Any time the plant is dormant these can be dug up, separated, and replanted to increase the number of plants.

Runners

Plants that send out runners may be the easiest to propagate of all. Just dig up new plants that appear around the mother plant, and snip off the root that connects them to the original plant, taking care to leave several inches of root attached to the new plant. Replant, either in pots or directly into the garden, keeping well watered until new growth appears.

Planting and Transplanting

Once you've prepped your garden plot, decided which herbs you want to grow and have put a plan to paper, it is time for the actual planting. Timing is important. Most perennials can be planted by mid-spring, while most annuals can only be planted after all danger of frost is past (May 20 in Northern Ohio). There are always exceptions. Both dill and cilantro are annuals that can be planted a month before the last frost date. If you want to plant the majority of the garden at one time, plan on planting around the end of May.

To plant seeds, make a furrow in the soil, sprinkle the seeds in the furrow, and cover with soil. Tamp the soil lightly with the back of your hoe to insure good contact between soil and seed. Don't forget to mark the rows so you can keep down weeds while waiting for your seedlings to emerge. Water the soil lightly after your seeds are planted, and continue to water once a day until plants are visible. Use a gentle mist so the seeds will not get washed away. Seeds are sown at a depth of roughly 3x their diameter.

You are probably going to be setting out transplants as well. By following a few simple steps, your newly planted herbs will soon be growing vigorously. The best time to set transplants in the garden is late afternoon. There will be less stress put on them if they don't have to deal with a full day's sun. Water them thoroughly a couple of hours before transplanting. When you remove the seedling from its pot, handle it only by the roots or leaves.

If the roots are compacted tightly together (root bound), you'll have to loosen them before planting. If left as they are, the roots will continue to grow this way and growth will be impaired. Think of the roots as terribly tangled hair that must be combed. You can use scissors, a fork, a small screwdriver, a stick, or even your hands to loosen the roots. Loosen them gently, being careful not to break the plant off from the roots. A few roots will get broken, but don't worry, they'll grow back.

Now you can dig the hole for your transplants. Dig the hole a little bigger than the pot in which the herb was growing. Pour about a cup of water into each hole and then set in the plant, firming the soil around it. Large plants may need 2 cups of water. The herb should be planted to the same depth at which it was growing, or a little deeper. Don't plant if the soil is too wet, it will dry into hard clumps that will impede the growth of the plant.

Maintenance

After your herb garden is planted you should have very few problems maintaining it. Herbs are pretty sturdy plants, rarely bothered by insects or disease. The same essential oils that give herbs their fragrance and flavor also seem to make them unattractive to most insects.

One of the diseases that can occur on herbs is rust. Rust disease can be spread if plants are touched when their leaves are wet. For this reason, stay out of your herb garden in the morning when plants are still wet from dew. Also avoid working in your garden right after a rainstorm, or watering.

You will have to control the growth of weeds throughout the season. One method is to cultivate the soil with a hoe, being careful not to damage the roots of your herb plants. Pull larger weeds by hand, getting as much of the root as possible.

To control weeds you might also choose to use mulch. Mulches are soil coverings that reduce or prevent the growth of weeds by posing a physical barrier. Some things that can be used as mulches are black plastic, agripaper, bark chips, peanut hulls, straw, hay, grass clippings, newspapers and even carpet scraps. While all of these mulches are effective in weed control, most would make poor choices for your herb garden. Why? Because in an herb garden you should consider appearance as well as function. Mulches like black plastic, carpeting and newspaper aren't very attractive, and will detract from the beauty of your plants. If you decide to mulch, go to your local garden center and pick out something that is pretty and useful.

Mulches should be applied to soil that is weed free. In addition to reducing weed growth, mulches also help to retain moisture in the soil. Normally, this is a good thing. However, if your soil is heavy or poorly drained, mulches can be counter-productive by keeping the soil too wet.

Whether you decide to use mulches or to weed by hand, it is always easier to control weeds when they are small. Also, as your herbs grow, they'll cover more ground, shading the soil, meaning fewer weeds for you to pull as the season progresses.

Once your herbs are growing, you should not need to water them very often. Most prefer dry soil, anyway. When plants are young, or after more than 10 days without rain, you may need to water. Water herbs during the middle of the day. This will give the leaves a chance to dry off before the sun sets. Leaves that are wet after dark are more likely to get diseases. If you water at ground level, rather than sprinkling the leaves, time of day is less important.

Harvest and Storage

Once your herbs are well established in the garden, you'll want to start harvesting them. When harvesting herbs don't pick more than one third of the total foliage at one time. Excessive pruning can be stressful to your plants. The essential oils in herbs are at their best flavor on warm, sunny days. Whenever possible, harvest your herbs in late morning to early afternoon, and always when the leaves are dry.

Plant leaves will be more flavorful and tender when plants are not in bloom. With annual plants, like basil, keep flowers trimmed off to extend harvest and to keep the leaves top quality. With perennials, you can wait to harvest leaves after flowering is finished, or you can trim off the blooms as you did with the annuals. With chives, always harvest the leaves at the soil line to encourage new growth.

Having fresh herbs for cooking is a real joy, but even a small garden will provide enough surplus herbs for storage and later use. Fresh herbs can be stored by freezing or drying.

Herbs can be frozen a couple of ways. You can simply chop the herbs and place them in a freezer container, label, and freeze. You can also mix herbs in a blender or food processor with a little water. Poor this mixture into ice cube trays and freeze. When frozen, the cubes can be transferred to freezer bags until you need them. Make sure that you use containers that are labeled for freezer use, or the smell of the herbs will permeate the whole freezer. For best flavor, use these herbs within 1 year of freezing, although they'll be safe to use for years.

The easiest way to dry herbs is to hang them upside down to air dry. Hang them up where it is warm, dry and dark. Attics and crawl spaces work well. Herbs dried in sunlight will lose some of their color and flavor.

Tie herbs together with rubber bands that way as the stems shrink during drying; the bands will contract and hold them firm. Seed heads can also be hung to dry, but put a paper bag over the seed head to catch seeds as they ripen and fall off. Put holes in the sides of the bag to allow good air circulation. Seed heads can also be air-dried on food safe screening.

Herbs can also be dried in convection ovens and dehydrators, according to manufacturer's instructions. Herbs can be dried in microwave ovens, as long as the quantities are small, and as long as there is something in the oven to absorb extra microwaves. A potato works well. It will absorb extra microwaves without giving off too much moisture.

Not all herbs keep their flavor when dried. Both chervil and cilantro change flavor drastically when dried, and should only be used fresh or frozen. Dried herbs should be stored in as whole a condition as possible. Crumble them just as you are about to use them. Also, store them away from heat and light to retain flavor. If your herbs are in clear jars, store them in a cupboard, rather than on a spice rack. The flavor of dried herbs is at its best when used within 1 year. The luxury of growing your own herbs is that you'll have fresh herbs every year, to replace what you've stored from the year before.

Plant and Seed Resource List

A Few of My Favorite Places

Some places need more than just a listing. These are the resources and people that are worth the effort to find and enjoy. Some have also become friends. Because many of these are seasonal industries, please call for hours beforehand.

Blue Stone Perennials

7211 Middleridge Rd.

Madison, OH 44057

1-440-428-7535

http://www.BlueStonePerennials.com

Unusual perennials can be found here along with all the regulars. Great assortment and a one-day sale every year that is not to be believed.

Graf Growers

1015 White Pond Dr.

Akron, OH 44320

1-330-836-2727

http://www.GrafGrowers.com/

The best sweet corn in the world. You also get a wonderful full line of plants and garden products with a warm family atmosphere and expert staff. A treasure.

Grace Brothers Nursery & Supply

12905 Ridge Road
North Royalton
1-440-237-2577

Grace Brothers Farm, Garden & Pet

1907 W. 65th St.
Cleveland
1-216-513-3262
http://www.GraceBrosNursery.com/

Great selection of fresh plants and dried materials. Helpful staff and some of the most creative planters anywhere. Fun gift shop.

Quailcrest Farm

2800 Armstrong Rd.

Wooster, OH 44691

1-330-345-6722

http://www.Quailcrest.com/

Impressive gardens and an awesome collection of plants for sale. You can always find more room for a new plant. Inspirational.

Caprilands Herb Farm

534 Silver St.

Coventry, CT 06238

1-860-742-7244

http://www.Caprilands.com/

Lily of the Valley Herb Farm

3969 Fox Ave.

Minerva, OH 44657

1-330-862-3920

http://www.LovHerbsnFlowers.com/

More than just herbs you can find a wealth of unusual perennials and expert help. What a treasure and well worth the trip.

Companion Plants

7247 North Coolville Ridge Rd.

Athens, OH 45701

1-740-592-4643

http://www.CompanionPlants.com/

Corso's Flower & Garden Center

3404 Milan Rd.

Sandusky, OH 44870

1-419-626-0789

http://www.Corsos.com/

Dean's Greenhouse

3984 Porter Rd.

Westlake, OH 44145

1-440 871-2050

http://www.DeansGreenhouse.com/

Hill Haven Farm & Greenhouse

7842 Center Rd.
Valley City, OH 44280
1-330-483-3233
http://www.HillHavenFloristAndGreenhouse.com/

Logee's Greenhouse

141 North St.
Danielson, CT 06239
1-860-774-8038
http://www.Logees.com/

Lowes Greenhouse

16540 Chillicothe Rd
Chagrin Falls, OH 44022
1-440-543-5123
http://www.LowesGreenhouse.com/

Nichols Garden Nursery

1190 Old Salem Rd. NE
Albany, Oregon 97321
1-541-928-9280
http://www.NicholsGardenNursery.com

Victory Seeds

http://www.VictorySeeds.com

Geo. W. Park Seed Co.

Greenwood, S.C. 29646

1-864-223-7333

http://ParkSeed.com/

Rosby Bros. Greenhouse

42 E. Schaaf Rd.

Brooklyn Hts., OH 44131

1-216-351-0850

http://www.RosbyCompanies.com/

Territorial Seed Company

PO Box 158
Cottage Grove, OR 97424
Phone Orders: 800-626-0866
Fax Orders: 888-657-3131

1-800-626-0866

http://www.TerritorialSeed.com/

I look forward to getting their catalog every year.

Baker Creek Heirloom Seeds

1-417-924-8917

http://www.RareSeeds.com

Heirloom Seeds

1-888-672 9202

http://www.HeirloomSeeds.com

About the Author

Judi Strauss began her career working for the horticulture department at the Extension office in Cuyahoga County. She specialized in urban gardening and designed and maintained the herb garden used for demonstration and teaching. She also lived on an herb farm.

She has written two books on herbs: "The Charmed Garden" on growing herbs and "The Charmed Kitchen" on cooking with herbs and spices. She is also the author of numerous cookbooks.

She currently lectures on a variety of gardening subjects including herbs, organic gardening, perennials and composting. She has lectured on "The History of Herbs" for the Cleveland Museum of Art as part of the grand re-opening of Armor Court and has also lectured at the Cleveland Botanical Gardens, where she has also worked.

Judi also teaches cooking classes and has a line of herbal products.

http://www.TheCharmedKitchen.com

www.ingramcontent.com/pod-product-compliance
Lightning Source LLC
Chambersburg PA
CBHW060342080526
44584CB00013B/888